CALUMET CITY PUBLIC LIBRARY

3 1613 00331 2330

W9-AJN-315

S
972.95
REY

S /46 23.50 164

A to Z Puerto Rico

BY JEFF REYNOLDS

children's press

A Division of Scholastic Inc.
New York Toronto London Auckland Sydney
Mexico City New Delhi Hong Kong
Danbury, Connecticut

CALUMET CITY PUBLIC LIBRARY

Consultant: Laird W. Bergad, Center for Latin American, Caribbean, and Latino Studies,
    The Graduate Center, The City University of New York
Series Design: Marie O'Neill
Photo Research: Candlepants Incorporated

For Randy Sue Latimer — J.R.

The photos on the cover show an anolis lizard (top left), a bastion of El Morro Fort
(top right), a stem of heliconia rostrata, also called hanging lobster claw (bottom right),
and a girl in traditional Puerto Rican dress (center).

Photographs © 2004: AP/Wide World Photos: 12 center (Ricky Arduengo), 12 bottom
(Andres Leighton); Archive Photos/Getty Images/Ana Martinez/Reuters: 23 top; Art
Resource, NY/Erich Lessing/Musee d'Orsay, Paris: 15 right; Bruce Coleman Inc.: 10 bottom,
26 (Mark Bacon), 36 (Werner Bertsch), 4 left, 5 right (Wendell Metzen); Corbis Images: 9
left, 24 bottom (Tony Arruza), 30 (Tom Bean), 13 top, 23 bottom (Bettmann), 15 left
(Mitchell Gerber), 17 top (Dave G. Houser), 29 (Kit Kettle), cover center, 6 top, 7, 8, 9 right,
10 top, 19, 34 bottom (Bob Krist), 6 bottom (Danny Lehman), 25 bottom, 28 left, 34 top
(Stephanie Maze), 35 top (Charles O'Rear), 14, 28 right (Reuters), cover bottom right, cover
top right (Royalty-Free), cover top left, 5 bottom (Kevin Schafer); D. Donne Bryant Stock
Photography/Suzanne L. Murphy: 32; Getty Images/Michael Massey: 22;
ImageState/ImageSource: 17 bottom; Mark Bacon: 37 bottom; PictureQuest: 24 top, 25 top
(Steve Dunwell), 11 (Wendell Metzen), 27, 33 (Timothy O'Keefe), 31 (Sarah Putnam); Puerto
Rico Stock: 12 top; Robertstock.com/J. Neubauer: 37 top; Stock Montage, Inc.: 13 bottom;
Taxi/Getty Images/Suzanne Murphy: 16 bottom; The Image Bank/Getty Images/Steve
Dunwell: 16 top; The Image Works: 35 bottom (Tony Arruza), 5 top (Avampini/V&W), 18
(Sven Martson); The Metropolitan Museum of Art: 38 (The Michael C. Rockefeller
Memorial Collection, Bequest of Nelson A. Rockefeller, 1979 (1979.206.380),
Photograph ©1981).
Map by XNR Productions

Library of Congress Cataloging-in-Publication Data

Reynolds, Jeff E., 1958-
  Puerto Rico / by Jeff Reynolds.— 1. ed.
      p. cm. — (A to Z)
 Includes bibliographical references and index.
Contents: Animals – Buildings – Cities – Dress – Exports – Food –
Government – History – Important people – Jobs – Keepsakes – Land
– Map – Nation – Only in Puerto Rico – People – Question – Religion –
School and sports – Transportation – Unusual Places – Visiting the
Country – Window to the past – X-tra special things – Yearly
Festivals – Zemi – Let's Explore More.
  Includes bibliographical references and index.
  ISBN 0-516-23656-3 (lib. bdg.)   0-516-25073-6 (pbk.)
 1. Puerto Rico—Juvenile literature. I. Title. II. Series.
  F1958.3.R49 2004
  972.95—dc22

                                2004009617

©2004 by Scholastic Inc.
All rights reserved. Published simultaneously in Canada.
Printed in the United States of America.
CHILDREN'S PRESS and associated logos are trademarks and or registered trademarks of
Scholastic Library Publishing. SCHOLASTIC and associated logos are trademarks and or
registered trademarks of Scholastic Inc.
1 2 3 4 5 6 7 8 9 10 R 13 12 11 10 09 08 07 06 05 04

Contents

Puerto Rican boas slither around in Puerto Rico, too. They grow to be about 7 feet (2 m) long.

The coquí grows to be only about 1 1/2 inches (4 cm) long.

Animals

Many animals, birds, and reptiles can be found on the island of Puerto Rico.

Manatee

The **coquí** is a tiny tree frog found everywhere in Puerto Rico. Its name comes from the sound it makes. It chirps, "koh-kee!"

Manatees are on the island, too. They are large underwater mammals. They feed on water plants and come to the surface to breathe.

The Puerto Rican parrot is **endangered**. There are less than one hundred of them left.

There are horses, too. People on the island are proud of their *paso fino* horses. The ancestors of these horses were brought to the island by Spanish explorers.

The Puerto Rican parrot is very rare.

5

Buildings

Bright colors make buildings in San Juan beautiful.

Some buildings in Puerto Rico are hundreds of years old. Others are very modern. When people from Spain began to come to the island, they built large homes with courtyards and public **plazas**. Some of these can still be seen today. Visitors to Puerto Rico are sometimes amazed to see the many beautiful colors of the island's buildings. A city block can look like an entire rainbow of colors!

6

Cities

San Juan is a large modern city with many hotels.

San Juan is Puerto Rico's largest city. It is also the island's capital. Part of the city is known as Old San Juan. It is a protected **historic site**. Puerto Ricans have worked hard to keep it looking the way it did long ago. It is also a popular spot for tourists. They enjoy walking along its blue-brick streets.

After San Juan, the cities of Ponce, Caguas, Carolina, and Bayamón are the most populated.

Girls in traditional costumes

Dress

Today, there is very little difference between the way people dress in Puerto Rico and the way people dress in the United States.

Holidays and celebrations are a reason to dress in the style of earlier times.

Loose-fitting clothes are the most comfortable for the island's warm climate.

Traditional clothing in Puerto Rico looks much the same as clothing worn during the island's days as a Spanish colony. Peasant blouses, often worn off the shoulders, are popular among women and girls. Long full skirts in bright colors complete the outfit. Men and boys will sometimes dress in the style of the *jíbaros*, or peasant farmers. Their wide-brimmed straw hat is known as a *pava*. Puerto Ricans often wear traditional clothing during celebrations.

Laboratories that make medicines must be kept very clean

Exports

Puerto Rico's most important exports are **pharmaceuticals**. Pharmaceuticals are medicines and other items used to treat illnesses and injuries. Most of the food that is raised in Puerto Rico feeds its growing population. Still, some crops can be exported. Among them are different types of fruit, such as **plantains** and pineapples. Other exports include electronics, chemicals, and coffee.

Pineapples

Limbers Recipe

WHAT YOU NEED:

• Approximately 1 1/2 cups of your favorite fruit juice

HOW TO MAKE IT:

Pour the juice into an ice cube tray. Carefully place the tray in the freezer. After the cubes have frozen, break one out of the tray. Save the others to eat later. You can add limbers to your favorite drink for a completely new taste. Experiment with juices you might not drink very often. Have you discovered a new favorite?

You can buy fresh fruit to make limbers at fruit stands, such as this one, throughout Puerto Rico.

Food

Limbers are a popular treat in Puerto Rico. They are frozen fruit juices. Mangos, guavas, coconut, and pineapple are the most common flavors, but limbers can be made from any kind of juice.

Ask an adult to join you in making the recipe above. It could be fun!

3 1613 00331 2330

CALUMET CITY PUBLIC LIBRARY

The Capitol Building in San Juan

Government

Governor Calderón

Aníbal Acevedo Vilá is Puerto Rico's resident commissioner in Washington, D.C.

Puerto Rico elects a governor every four years. Governors choose other leaders to help them in their duties. Puerto Rico elected its first woman governor in 2000. Her name is Sila María Calderón.

The island has a constitution, a court system, and a legislative assembly that is similar to the United States Congress. Puerto Ricans also elect a lawmaker to send to Washington, D.C., to serve in the U.S. House of Representatives. This person is known as the resident commissioner. The resident commissioner does not participate in the final votes that set laws for the United States.

History

The arrival of Columbus in 1493

Juan Ponce de León

Christopher Columbus arrived in what is now Puerto Rico in 1493. It was his second voyage to the New World. He named the island San Juan Bautista, which means St. John the Baptist. In his journal, Columbus called the island and the town he started there Puerto Rico, which means "rich port." Soon Puerto Rico became the name by which the island was known.

Puerto Rico became a Spanish colony, and the famous explorer Juan Ponce de León was its first governor. The Spanish used Puerto Rico as a stopping place for ships going to other places in North and South America. Puerto Rico was a colony of Spain until 1898.

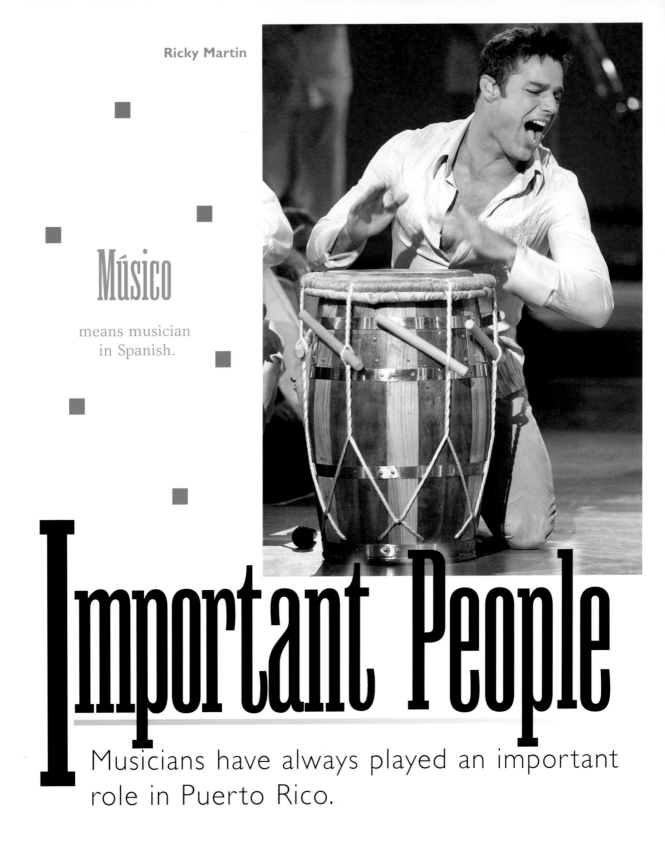

Músico

means musician
in Spanish.

Important People

Musicians have always played an important
role in Puerto Rico.

Rita Moreno is an Academy Award-winning actress and singer who was born in Humacao.

The Student by Francisco Oller

Ricky Martin was born in San Juan. He began his career singing in a boy group called Menudo. He is now a solo artist and the top-selling Latin performer.

Rita Moreno is another well-known Puerto Rican signer. She also dances and acts. She is famous for her roles in the movies *The King and I* and *West Side Story*.

Many artists come from Puerto Rico, too. Francisco Oller was a well-known Puerto Rican painter. He was born in Bayamón in 1833. Oller studied art in Spain and Paris. He died in 1917 in San Juan, Puerto Rico.

Jobs

These steel workers help build **Puerto Rico's** homes and offices.

Tourism is an important part of Puerto Rico's economy.

Many Puerto Ricans have jobs that provide services to tourists. They have jobs such as hotel and restaurant workers. About one-fifth of the workers in Puerto Rico are employed by the government. They have jobs in government offices. Some Puerto Ricans are self-employed or work in offices. Jobs in manufacturing employ more than one out of every ten workers.

Miguel Caraballo is one of Puerto Rico's leading makers of vejigante masks.

Keepsakes

Handmade masks are sold everywhere in Puerto Rico. They are a wonderful way to remember your visit to the island. Some of them are called **vejigante** masks. They are made from coconut shells, wood, or **papier-mâché**.

Some of the best keepsakes from Puerto Rico are absolutely free. Spend part of your time at the beach hunting for one perfect seashell!

17

El Yunque Rain Forest

Land

Puerto Rico's nickname is the "Isle of Enchantment." Puerto Rico is made up of one large island and many small ones.

Beautiful sandy beaches can be found along the main island's north and south coasts. Most of the island, however, is covered with hills and mountains. The Cordillera Central Mountain Range stretches for most of the length of the island. Many of the forests that once covered its hillsides have been cut down to make room for farms and people. In some parts of the island, it rains almost every day. Beautiful flowers and other rain forest plants grow in those areas.

Isla

means island in Spanish.

19

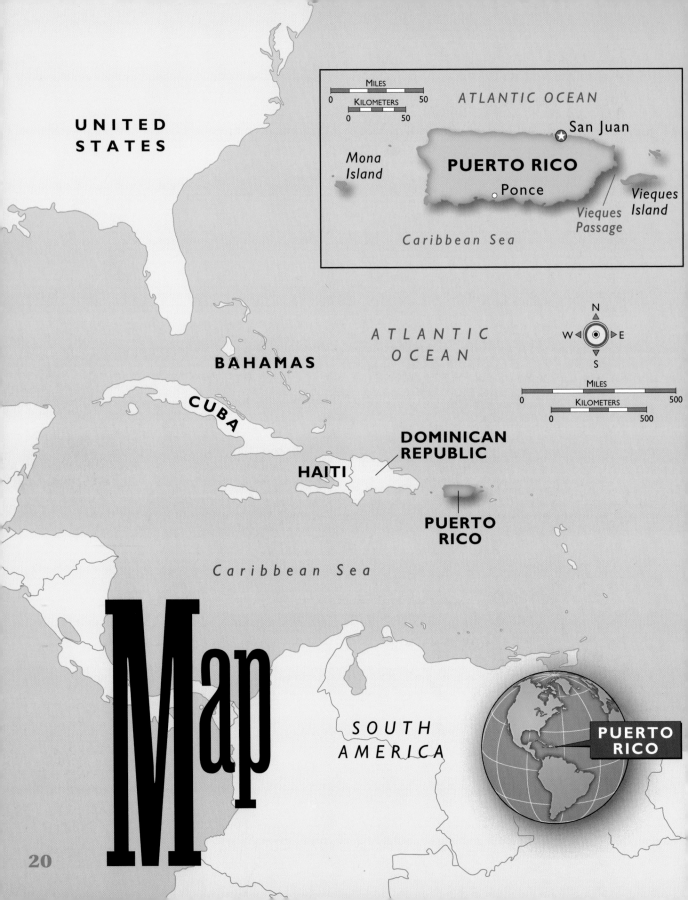

MILES
0   50
KILOMETERS
0   50

ATLANTIC OCEAN

San Juan

Mona Island

PUERTO RICO

Ponce

Vieques Island

Vieques Passage

Caribbean Sea

UNITED STATES

ATLANTIC OCEAN

N
W   E
S

MILES
0   500
KILOMETERS
0   500

BAHAMAS

CUBA

DOMINICAN REPUBLIC

HAITI

PUERTO RICO

Caribbean Sea

Map

SOUTH AMERICA

PUERTO RICO

Nation

Bandera

(BAN-dehrr-ah)
means flag or banner
in Spanish.

The flag of Puerto Rico has three red stripes, two white stripes, and a white star in the middle of a blue triangle. It has been the country's flag since 1952, when Puerto Rico became a commonwealth associated with the United States. **Commonwealth** is a word that means "having to do with." Some Puerto Ricans would like their country to become the 51st state. Others would like it to become more independent of the United States.

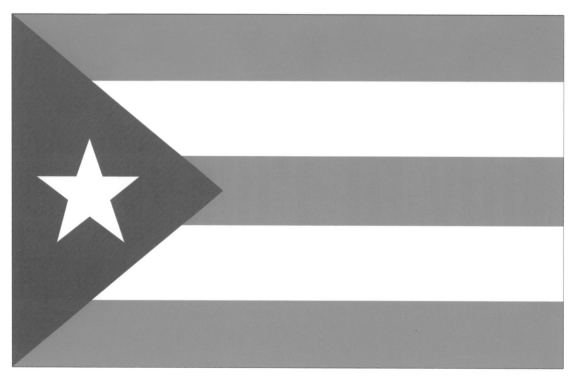

ABRÁZATE A PUERTO RICO
JUVENTUD INDEPENDENTISTA

Only in Puerto Rico

In some ways, the Commonwealth of Puerto Rico is like any state in the United States. In other ways, it is very different.

Some of the voters in Puerto Rico do not want it to become the 51st state.

Puerto Ricans are U.S. citizens, but they do not have many of the rights that Americans enjoy. They cannot vote for the U.S. President. However, they can serve in the U.S. military.

Still, there are benefits for Puerto Ricans. They do not pay taxes to the United States. They are allowed to move freely between Puerto Rico and the United States. In addition, the United States provides money to the island for schools, roads, and the other things that it needs.

Luis Muñoz Marín helped Puerto Rico to become more independent.

People

Nearly four million people live in Puerto Rico. Most have ancestors who were Spanish or a mixture of European, African, or **Taíno Indian**.

Families are an important part of
Puerto Rican life.

Puerto Ricans are proud to have such a
rich **heritage**. All of these cultures can be
felt in Puerto Rico today. Spanish is spoken
more often than English. African rhythms
can be heard in the island's music. Some
Puerto Ricans look very much like their
Taíno ancestors. *Trigueños* is a word for
people who have a mix of European,
African, and Indian ancestors. They are the
majority of the island's population.

Many children in Puerto Rico
have godparents.

25

Brown bats in a Mona Island cave

Question

What was the "Treasure of Mona Island?"

Mona Island is west of Puerto Rico's main island. It was once used by pirates. But Mona Island's treasure was not buried by pirates. It was left by bats!

The island's many caves are home to thousands of bats. The floors of these caves were once thick with bat droppings. At the end of the 19th century, a group of men removed the droppings. They sold it as a fertilizer called **guano** and became very rich.

San Juan Cathedral

Religion

About 85 percent of Puerto Ricans are Roman Catholic. They follow the Christian teachings of the Roman Catholic religion. Catholicism was brought to Puerto Rico by priests who traveled with the early Spanish explorers. For many years, Protestant (non-Catholic) churches were not allowed in Puerto Rico. That began to change in the 1800s. Today, 15 percent of Puerto Ricans are Protestant or belong to other religions.

A double play during the Caribbean World Series

School friends in San Juan

School & Sports

Schools in Puerto Rico follow the same education laws followed by schools in the United States. Like U.S. schools, they receive money from the federal government. In Puerto Rico, both Spanish and English are required subjects.

Baseball is very popular in Puerto Rico. The champion of its six-team professional league plays in the Caribbean World Series, against teams from Mexico, Venezuela, and the Dominican Republic. Many Puerto Rican players join teams in the United States. The most famous of them was Roberto Clemente, who played for the Pittsburgh Pirates.

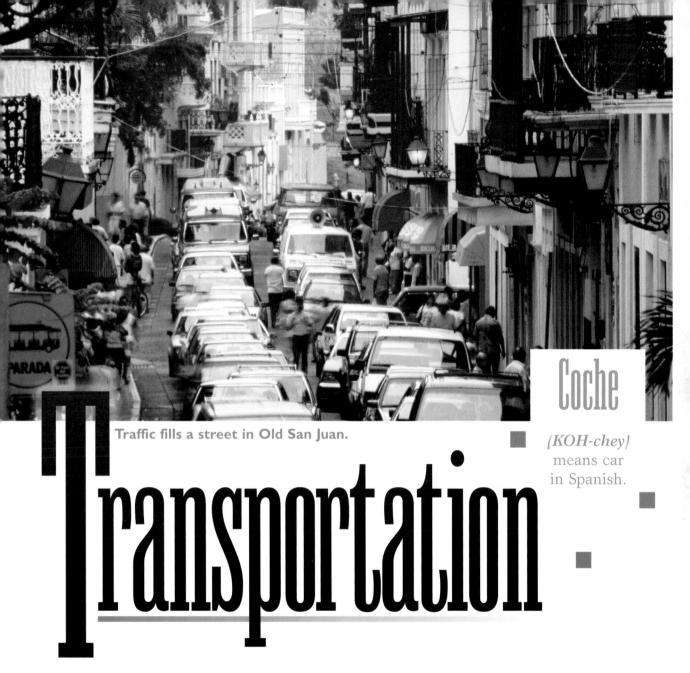

Traffic fills a street in Old San Juan.

Transportation

Coche

(KOH-chey) means car in Spanish.

One major highway circles the shoreline of Puerto Rico. Other roads crisscross the mountains. Most people get around in automobiles. Streets in the cities, especially the old parts of cities, are often very crowded with cars.

No part of the island is very far from any other part. Because of this, the island does not have a network of railroads and airports like other places. Still, many planes fly to Puerto Rico from the United States and other countries.

Caguana Indian Ceremonial Park

Unusual Places

The Taíno Indians played a game that was similar to modern soccer. Teams were made up of several people. Both men and women played the game. Winning the game was thought to bring people good luck. The game was such an important part of their lives that they built special areas in which to play it. One of these ancient ball courts can still be seen at the Caguana Indian Ceremonial Park.

30

Counting the eggs of a leatherback turtle

Visiting the Country

Tortuga

(TOR-too-gah)
**means turtle
in Spanish.**

When you visit the beach in Puerto Rico, you might be asked to do some life-saving. You won't be saving human lives. You'll be saving turtle lives!

Leatherbacks are very large turtles that come ashore in Puerto Rico to lay their eggs. There are not many leatherbacks left. Volunteers help baby leatherbacks get safely from their nests to the ocean. This means that there will be more babies that can grow into adults in their ocean home.

31

Modern Puerto Ricans in clothing like that worn by the Taíno.

Window to the Past

Many thousands of Taíno Indians lived on Puerto Rico when Columbus arrived. Within about fifty years, almost all of them died from diseases brought over by explorers.

A recreation of a Taíno hut

The Taíno's name for their home was *Borinquen*. They lived in villages made up of huts that surrounded a large courtyard. They grew or caught the food that they ate. They traded with people on neighboring islands for the other things they needed.

The Taíno were forced to become slaves by the Spanish new-comers. Many Taíno died from the harsh work. Others died from diseases brought to the island by the Europeans.

As the Taíno began to disappear, slaves from Africa were brought to the island.

Arecibo Observatory

X-tra Special Things

The Parque de Bombas is a firefighting museum.

El Morro

The underground caves near Aguas Buenas are a spectacular sight.

Puerto Ricans may be the first to know if there is life in outer space. In the northwest part of the island there is a giant telescope called the Arecibo Observatory. It's not used for seeing; it listens for sounds in space.

One of the most unusual sights on the island is the Parque de Bombas in Ponce. This old firehouse is painted in stripes of yellow, black, red, and green!

Puerto Rico's most famous building is an old fortress called El Morro. It was built by the Spanish in 1539. They used it to defend San Juan Harbor from their enemies. Its round watch-towers are now the main symbol of the country.

Vejigante masks

Yearly Festivals

Las Navidades is Puerto Rico's Christmastime celebration. It begins in mid-December, and ends on January 6th.

Elaborate costumes and masks
are worn at Carnival time.

Las Navidades ends on
Three Kings Day, January 6th.

Las Navidades is the biggest celebration of the year, but other religious holidays—such as Easter and saints' days—are important, too. Holidays are a time for Puerto Ricans to visit family and friends and enjoy special meals together.

The nation also celebrates the anniversaries of special days in its history. March 11 is the date on which slavery was ended in 1873. November 19 is the date on which Columbus landed on the island. Both are holidays. Carnival is a late-winter festival held in Ponce and other cities. It's much like Mardi Gras in the United States.

Zemi

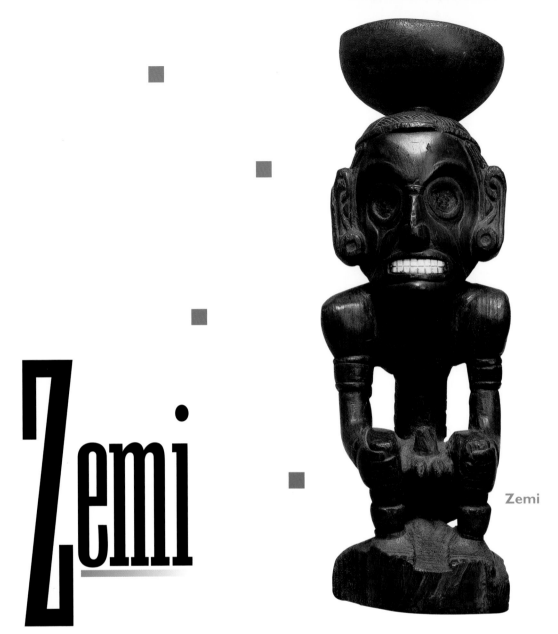

Zemi

Zemi is the name of a god that was worshipped by the Taíno Indians. They believed that good luck was the result of how happy Zemi was. To keep Zemi in a good mood, they would make offerings of food, drinks, and tobacco. The word zemi is also used to describe jewelry and other objects that were made to look like the god. Having a likeness of the god nearby showed that you were always thinking of Zemi.

Spanish and English Words

commonwealth a partnership between two countries

coquí (koh-KEE) a small tree frog found in Puerto Rico

endangered at risk of disappearing

guano (guah-NO) bat droppings used as fertilizer

heritage all of the things from our past that make us who we are, especially our ancestry

historic site a place set aside and protected because something important happened there

jíbaros (HEE-bah-rohs) peasant farmers from the mountains of Puerto Rico

limbers treats made from frozen fruit juice

papier-mâché (PAY-pur muh-SHAY) paper that is soaked in glue

paso fino (PASO FEE-noh) a breed of horse known for its delicate way of walking

pava (PAH-vah) a wide-brimmed straw hat worn by peasant farmers

pharmaceuticals chemical products used to treat illnesses, such as medicine

plantains a banana-like fruit, often fried and served like a vegetable

plazas large open areas or courtyards often used as public gathering places

Taíno Indians a group of Indians who lived on Puerto Rico and neighboring islands

Trigueños (tree-GAYNG-yohs) Puerto Ricans of mixed European, Taíno, and African ancestry

vejigante (veh-jee-HAHN-tay) a colorful, frightening character in Puerto Rican carnival celebration

Zemi a Taíno god

Let's Explore More

Children of Puerto Rico by Michael Elsohn Ross, Carolrhoda Books, 2002

Puerto Rico by Leila Merrell Foster, Heinemann Library, 2001

Puerto Rico, A True Book™ by Elaine Landau, Children's Press, 1999

Websites

http://Welcome.toPuertoRico.org/
Explore Puerto Rico from your computer. Discover the culture, people, government, history, and economy of the island.

http://www.henry.k12.ga.us/pges/kid-pages/islands/PuertoRico/default.htm
Discover fun and interesting facts on this website written by kids for kids.

Italic page numbers indicate illustrations.

Meet the Author

JEFF REYNOLDS was raised on a farm in Illinois. He has lived in Minneapolis-St. Paul, New York City, and Connecticut, and now lives and works in Washington, D.C. He received a B.A. from Western Illinois University and an M.A. in Theater History and Criticism from Brooklyn College. At various times he has been a farmer, milkman, school custodian, housepainter, hotel bellman, stamp dealer, teacher, librarian, actor, journalist, and editor. He is also the author of A to Z books about Egypt, Germany, Japan, and the United States.